C000130390

PUGLIA TRAVEL GUIDE

Where to Go & What to Do

LILY MARSH

Table of Contents

Puglia

Puglia forms the 'heel' of the famous 'boot' of Italy and offers 800 km of sunshine-drenched oceanfront, green olive groves and idyllic, baroque towns. Its Mediterranean-influenced cuisine provides visitors with an authentic and hugely enjoyable taste of Italy. The region's main towns include Bari, Taranto, Brindisi, Ostuni, and Lecce, each having a medieval flavor.

Located in the southeastern region of Italy, Puglia is an emerging tourist destination. The region has been frequented by cruise ships for decades as it is a port of call for those visiting Greece and the Albanian coast. Puglia's Latin name Apulia – often used in English also – is derived from a Greek word that means – 'the other side of the Adriatic'.

Puglia has been ruled by outsiders for the most part with the Greeks arriving in the 8th century BC. In the 3rd century BC, the Romans took over, attracted by the vast resources of olive oil, wheat, and wine.

So important was the Puglia region to the Romans, that they built the Via Appia to link Puglia with Rome. It was under the Roman Emperor Frederick II in the 13th century that the Puglia region flourished. From art to architecture, the Puglia region saw a huge rise in its fortunes. The following centuries brought a lot of turmoil for Puglia. Between the 13th and 19th centuries, it was occupied or ruled by the French, Turks, Austrians, and the Spanish, until it joined united Italy in 1861. While, on one hand the invasions brought a lot of political strife, on the other hand, it gave Puglia an eclectic mix of culture and cuisine, something that has given the region a distinct identity.

Puglia has six regions: Bari (the capital of the province), Foggia, Brindisi, Lecce, Taranto, and Barletta-Andria-Trani. The region spans 20,000 sq km and has low-lying hills, plains, a vast plateau and a long stretch of Mediterranean coastline.

Puglia has something of interest for every visitor. For the spiritual, there are many historic churches and colorful festivals. Nature lovers can choose from numerous natural parks or even the wild nature. Puglia also has many walking, cycling, and trekking trails. Many of the major towns of Puglia have a medieval old town where one can see beautiful Baroque castles and houses. With a number of hotels, seaside villas, and inns coming up in the recent years, Puglia offers a wide variety of leisure and comfort for visitors from across the globe.

Customs & Culture

The Puglia cultural calendar is filled with festivals and events throughout the year ranging from historical re-enactments and religious events to culinary festivals and traditional celebrations.

The Putignano Carnival in February and March is not only one of the longest carnivals, but, according to many, is also the oldest carnival in the world. The 2-month long carnival is a mix of religious and social events and includes four major parades during the last week of February and the first 2 weeks of March. Easter is celebrated with a lot of fanfare, especially in Bari and Gallipoli. In Bari, during the 'procession of the Cross' more than 100 crosses are carried across town by devotees with thorn-crowns on their heads. Gallipoli has a number of processions on Maundy Thursday and Good Friday.

The summer month of May starts in Taranto with the Festival of San Cataldo. Held at the canal near the historical center of the city, the festival includes a procession with the statue of the patron Saint San Cataldo. A similar festival in Bari during the same time is the Festival of San Nicola. Both these festivals conclude with spectacular fireworks. Lecce celebrates the La Festa di SS Maria and the Truffle Food Festival in May. While the former is a series of musical events, the latter is a food festival in the Otranto historic center. Food lovers will also enjoy the Negroamaro Wine Festival and the San Pietro e Paolo food festival in Lecce every June.

There are a lot of music festivals in the summer months. In Taranto, there are the Festival Della Valle d'Itria and International Folklore Festival. In Lecce, there is the annual International Jazz Festival. The Locus Music Festival in Bari also sees a number of renowned jazz musicians from all over the world. Brindisi celebrates music through the Aperitivo Classico – a classical music festival, and the Sagra Di Feragosto – a festival with pizzica musicians and dancers.

Historical re-enactments can be seen in events like the La Scamiciata (Brindisi), Mottola AD 1102 (Taranto), Torneo dei Rioni (Brindisi), and the Challenge of Barletta (Barletta).

The Puglia region is well known for its arts and crafts. The Ceramic from Grottaglie has been famous from the medieval times. Traditional ceramic making is still displayed to the public at the Ceramics Quarter. Wrought iron products were popular in the Salento region for many centuries. Salento region is also popular for papier-mâché which can still be seen in Massafra, Putignano, and Lecce. Lecce is also famous for its limestone, which has been used for centuries to make statues and sculptures. Rutigliano in Bari is famous for its terracotta products, especially the 'terracotta whistle'. Those visiting the city in January can witness the traditional 'Whistle Feast'.

Geography

The Puglia region is bordered by Campania province in the west, Molise in the north, and Basilicata in the southwest. The long stretch of the east coast faces the Adriatic Sea and neighbors the countries of Greece, Albania, Croatia, Bosnia-Herzegovina, and Montenegro. The closest major city to the province-capital Bari is Naples (222 km). The capital Rome is at a distance of about 374 km.

The Puglia region is primarily served by 2 airports. The Bari Airport, also known as Bari Palese – http://www.aeroportodibari.com/ - IATA: BRI – is located about 8 km west of the town center and is the most important airport of Puglia. This international airport has a number of connections with many major European cities like London, Munich, Prague, Brussels, and Athens. There is also a weekly direct connection with New York City. The airport operates both regular and low cost airlines like Ryanair, Easyjet, and Helvetic. The cheapest way to get to the city is through the public bus service. A slightly more expensive and quicker service is provided by the airport shuttle. The buses terminate at the Piazza Aldo Moro near the railway station which is ideal for visitors who are having an onward journey from Bari.

For those planning to reach Bari by bus can use the services from Onbus

Company - http://www.onbus.it/Avvia.rtm, or Eurolines Touring - http://www.eurolines.de/de/startseite/. Train services are available through Trenitalia. Details of schedules and ticket prices can be found at - http://www.onbus.it/Avvia.rtm.

For those looking for a more scenic travel can opt for the ferries from neighboring Greece (Patra port), Albania (Durres), Croatia (Dubrovnik), or Montenegro (Kotor). Details of these international ferry services along with ticket prices and schedules can be found at - http://www.ferries.gr/.

The Brindisi Airport - http://www.brindisiairport.net/; IATA: BDS - is located further south and is ideal for those planning to visit Brindisi or Lecce. Serving the Salento region, the airport is officially called Aeroporto del Salento. Flights are few in this small airport but there are direct connections to cities in Italy, UK, France, Germany, and Switzerland. There are bus services connecting the airport to the town of Brindisi including one that stops close to the railway station. There is also a direct bus connection to neighboring Lecce. The Brindisi Airport has limited services with the public transport operating until 11:30pm; those planning to arrive later should take the taxi or make prearrangements for a pick-up service. Brindisi is also connected by an international ferry service with Corfu (Greece).

The best way to reach Lecce is through the Brindisi Airport. However, for those who are already in Italy and wish to take the train can do so from cities like Naples, Venice, Rome, Milan, and Bari. The station is only a km from the town center but taxis are expensive; it is recommended to contact the hotel for a pick-up service.

Other Puglia regions like Foggia and Taranto are best reached by train. However, it can be noted that there are smaller airports in Taranto and Foggia - http://www.aeroportidipuglia.it/index.asp, with limited domestic flights.

Transport infrastructure within the cities in the Puglia region is scarce. One can opt for taxis or rental cars. However, since most of these towns are small, one can easily cover most of the attractions by foot. The best way to travel from one Pugliese city to another is by train, or, if available, the ferry.

Weather & Best Time to Visit

The Pugliese region is identified with a Mediterranean climate having hot and dry summers and mild winters. The months between May and September are the warmest. Temperatures reach an average high of about 28 degrees Celsius. The average low in these months, range from 13 to 18 degrees Celsius. The winter months – between November and March – see the highest temperatures range between 13 to 17 degrees Celsius; the average low during these months hover between 5 to 7 degrees Celsius. Rainfall is almost evenly distributed throughout the year with the winter months being the wettest – with about 60 inches of monthly rainfall. The constant clear sunny Mediterranean weather makes the Puglia region an ideal tourist destination throughout the year.

Sights & Activities: What to See & Do

Bari

Capital of the Province of Bari and the Puglia region, the city of Bari is the 2nd most important city in mainland south Italy, after Naples. Once an important port city, Bari today, is an important base for the Puglia region for commerce, especially naval trade. Bari has a beautiful medieval town which has retained many of the Roman architecture. The city is an important node for tourism for the Puglia region, a fact that has prompted the Bari administration to improve the tourism infrastructure of the city. The focus is not only on getting better connections to the major tourist destinations in the Puglia region, but on the town itself. Better accommodation and nightlife are also being worked on to attract visitors for a longer stay.

Bari has its own airport and it also has a number of train connections from many Italian cities. In fact, different railway lines terminate in Bari. All these lines terminate in different stations near the Piazza Aldo Moro. International ferry services are available with a number of neighboring European countries. Within the city, one can use the public bus service run by AMTAB. However, attractions in Bari are not too far from each other and can be easily covered by foot.

Alberobello (Pug Girl, CC BY 2.0)

Basilica of Saint Nicholas

Bari is also known as the City of Saint Nicholas, after the patron saint of the city. The 11th century Basilica of Saint Nicholas located in the Old Town is one of the most revered places of pilgrimage for Orthodox Christians and Roman Catholics. Dedicated to the patron saint – also called Santa Claus – the church was specially built to house the relics of the saint. The relics were originally in the Turkish town of Myra, but were moved to Bari in the 11th century in line with the saint's wish to be buried in this city.

This Roman Catholic Church is built in a Romanesque style of architecture. The church, which looks more like a castle with its square appearance, has been used as a castle a number of times over the centuries. Beautiful arches, granite columns, and stunning Romanesque sculptures adorn the interior of the church. The church also has a very good collection of historic Roman paintings.

Bari Cathedral

Housing the relics of Saint Sabinus, the Bari Cathedral is a church, older to, but less famous than the Basilica of St Nicholas. The Church was built replacing the Imperial Byzantine Cathedral that was destroyed by William I of Sicily.

Ruins of the cathedral can still be seen under the nave of the present day church. The church is built in a typical Romanesque style of architecture that is unique to the Pugliese region. It has a simple pristine interior with 2 aisles and 16 columns. The relics of Saint Sabinus are kept in a large altar in the crypt. The façade of the church, made in a simple Romanesque form, has a large rose window adorned with fantasy figures.

Alberobello (Pug Girl, CC BY 2.0)

Castillo Svevo

Located close to the Bari Cathedral is the Castillo Svevo or the Swabian Castle. Built by the sea in the mid 12th century by the Normans, the castle today, is open to the public, and is used for exhibitions. Like some other buildings of importance, this castle was also destroyed by William I of Sicily but was rebuilt in 1233 by Frederick II – the Holy Roman Emperor. The castle was used as a prison when it was used by the King of Naples. It has moats on 3 sides and opens up to the sea on its fourth, the northern side.

Old Bari

Barivecchia to the locals, Old Bari is filled with alleys and passageways from the medieval times. The area has been upgraded in the recent years to attract tourists. Today, the area has a number of pubs and cafes where visitors can not only enjoy a drink but also enjoy the medieval atmosphere.

To the east of the Old Town is the Port Vecchio, the old port. Every morning fishermen bring in their catch in small wooden boats and sell the fish directly at the waterfront. In the same area are the 2 interlocking squares Piazza Mercantile and Piazza del Ferrarese with a number of restaurants, ideal to grab a quick lunch or snack. The white column in the square with a statue of a lion at its base, was once used to tie up and flog defaulting debtors.

Amphitheatre in Lecce (vic15, CC BY 2.0)

Petruzzelli Theater

Completed in 1903, the Petruzzelli Theater is the largest theater in the Puglia region and the 4th largest in Italy. The grandeur of this theater puts it at par with the other famous theaters in Italy, the San Carlo in Naples, and the La Scala in Milan. Host to many famous performances over the decades, the theater was almost completely gutted in a fire in 1991. It was reopened after 18 years, in 2009, after a multi-million dollar renovation. Other theaters in Bari include the Margherita Theater and the Piccinni Theater.

Pinacoteca Provinciale

Located on the sea front, this is not only the town art gallery but one of the most important galleries of art in the Puglia region. The gallery was established in 1928 and has an important collection of sculptures and paintings from the 11th to the 19th centuries.

Other places of interest in Bari include the archeological museum, the Russian Church, and the Santa Teresa dei Maschi – a 17th century Baroque church. Beach lovers can head to the Pane e Pomodoro Beach. For the shopaholics, there is the Murat City Center, considered the biggest shopping zone in the whole of Italy. Soccer lovers can head to catch a game at the 58000-seater Stadio San Nicola, an impressive stadium built for the 1990 FIFA World Cup.

Bari (Pandemia, CC BY 2.0)

Lecce

With a history of nearly 2500 years, the city of Lecce is one of the most important cities of the Salentine Peninsula, and of course, the region of Puglia. The city of Lecce – capital of the Lecce province, is located near the southern tip of the 'Italian heel'. It is often called the Florence of the South for its abundance of stunning Baroque architecture. Lecce, surrounded by its attractive countryside, beautiful villages, and the seashore, attracts a large number of tourists throughout the year. Such is the popularity of Lecce that many Europeans from nearby countries fly in to Lecce just for the weekend! The 2014 movie – Walking on Sunshine – was extensively shot in the Puglia region, especially Lecce, highlighting the beautiful white sand beaches and the Baroque masterpieces.

The city has a long affinity with the Greeks; in fact, a variant of the Greek language is still spoken in some parts of Lecce.

Lecce has been important over the years for the unique limestone that is found in the area. Still the primary export of the city, the 'Lecce stone' is popularly used for sculptures. Other important products from the area include olive oil and wine.

Old Town & Town Squares

Once in town, one of the major attractions is the old town center. A good way to start is to take the trenino – a mini tourist train. The hop-on hop-off train offers guided tours and passes through various parts of the center. 2 major squares in Lecce are the Piazza del Duomo and the Piazza Sant'Oronzo. The Duomo Square was built in the mid 12th century but the present look comes from the 17th century facelift which also saw the addition of the 70 m high bell tower. Here, one can also see the Roman amphitheater and the statue of the patron saint of Lecce, Sant'Oronzo.

Other places of interest include the mid 16th century Castle of Charles V. The castle, with its delicately ornamented interiors, was never used as a fortress but was used as a military district from time to time. In the 18th century, one of its rooms was transformed into a theater. Today, the castle is used for various exhibitions and cultural shows. One can also see the 16th century Sedile Palace, 17th century Palzzo dei Celistini, and the early 15th century Torre del Parco – the Park Tower.

Cisternino-Brindisi (ItaliaABC, CC BY 2.0)

Religious Buildings

Lecce is dotted with many religious buildings, one of the most important being the late 17th century Church of the Holy Cross. This Baroque church has an extremely decorated façade with intricate artwork, Corinthian columns, statues, and a large rose window. The décor of the interior matches that of the exterior with 17 altars, 2 aisles, and a nave. The coat of arms on the main altar is that of the Adomi family, who were once buried in the basilica. The church interior is also adorned with some paintings from the medieval period.

The towering Lecce Cathedral is the seat of the Archbishop of Lecce. Dedicated to the Assumption of the Virgin Mary, this church was originally built in the mid 12th century but rebuilt in 1659 under orders from Bishop Luigi Pappacoda. The relics of the bishop are kept in the altar of the church. Of the 2 entrances to the church, the northern façade has a simpler look; the second entrance facing the square is richly decorated with Baroque artwork. Notable on this façade are the statues of St Fortunatus, St Justus, and St Orontius. The interior, built on a Latin cross plan, similar to the Church of the Holy Cross, has 12 altars, 2 aisles, and a nave. The wooden ceiling has beautiful paintings from the Christian history including the Last Supper.

Other churches in Lecce include the 12th century San Nicolo and Cataldo Church, the 17th century Church of San Matteo, and the 16th century Theatines Church.

Brindisi

Brindisi is located in south Italy. Its natural port on the Adriatic shore has made the city an important point of commerce for many centuries. Brindisi's fortunes have always been intertwined with the countries on the other side of the Adriatic. Even today, not only is the Brindisi port an important trade zone for Middle East and Greece, it is also used extensively by tourists as a point of entry and exit. From the ancient times, the city was directly connected to Rome through the Appian Way. One of the tourist attractions in the city is the 19 m high column at the port, which was built to symbolize the end of the Appian Way.

Brindisi was founded by the Greeks but its fortunes and architecture flourished under the Roman rule. The city had to go through many decades of rebuilding after it was severely bombed in World War II. Fortunately, many of its ancient architectural treasures escaped the bombings. In the recent years, Brindisi, with its newly laid palm-tree-lined boulevards and revamped seaside promenade have given the city a youthful look. Coupled with its Baroque treasures, Brindisi surely demands a day or two from visiting travelers.

The main tourist attractions of Brindisi include the Castelo Svevo or Swabian Castle. This 13th century castle with 7 towers and high walls have played many roles, from being a royal residence to being a prison.

The 15th century Aragonese Castle or the Sea Fort is also located on the seafront. On the Appian Way one can see the Grand Fountain that was built by the Romans and restored in 1192. Brindisi has a number of churches. Notable amongst those are the 13th century Santa Maria del Casale Church and the 18th century Brindisi Cathedral. The Romanesque Church of San Benedetto, the Portico of the Templars, and the Victory Square are also popular tourist attractions in the city.

Brindisi is a delight for those looking for Italian cuisine. Although mostly popular for the Appia Wine and the Brindisi Olive Oil, the city also produces Limoncello – a lemon based liquor, Almond Milk, and a variety of cheese made from sheep milk.

Galipoli Seaside (Pug Girl, CC BY 2.0)

Taranto

Capital of the Province of Taranto, the city of Taranto is a coastal city located on the shore of the Gulf of Taranto on the Ionian Sea. Once an important military and commercial city, Taranto has, over the centuries, been ruled by many different kingdoms and dynasties. This has resulted in an eclectic mix of architectural styles visible throughout the city. The calmness and serenity of this city, marked by the numerous small fishing boats, is often contradicted by the large naval ships that are often harbored here for the strategic location.

Tourist attractions in the city include the 11th century Cathedral of San Cataldo. This Baroque cathedral with its beautiful façade and stunning mosaic floors houses the relics of the patron saint of the city, St Cataldo.

There is also a castle opposite which is the remains of a Greek Temple, one of the few remaining testimonies of this former Greek colony. Taranto also has a number of theaters and a growing nightlife scene. The narrow alleys of the historic center of Taranto transports one to the medieval days of this port city. The center is a great place to have a drink or to try some authentic south Italian seafood, especially the local delicacy – pasta with mussels.

Foggia

Capital of the province of Foggia, the city of Foggia is located on the northern part of Puglia. Also called the 'granary of Italy', the name means pit in Latin, denoting the pits where the wheat was stored. The city is built on the Tavoliere plain and has been an important source of agricultural produce to south Italy. Although Foggia differs from other popular Pugliese cities by not being a seaside resort; the beautiful landscape and Baroque architecture has a charm of its own.

One of the popular attractions is the Foggia Cathedral. Also known as the Church of St Mary, the present day Baroque church was built in the 18th century after the original 12th century collegiate church was destroyed in an earthquake. The historic 15th century Palazzo Dogana – Customs Building – is one of the oldest buildings in the city.

An important part of the Italian culture that has been recognized by UNESCO, this building houses the Gallery of Modern and Contemporary Art. Other places of interest include the Arch of Frederick II, the Church of the Crosses, the Piazza Cavour, and the Archeological Park at Passo di Corvo.

Foggia offers a cuisine that is unique to the Pugliese, or Apulian hinterland. Bruschetta, a type of hardened bread topped with tomatoes and olive oil is a must try. Also popular are the Pancotto – a bread soup, and maritata – a vegetable soup made with local fresh produce. One can also try the pizza and pasta, made with fresh local produce, which gives it a distinct and delicious taste.

Gelato! (Pug Girl, CC BY 2.0)

Tremiti Islands

Located about 40 km north from the coast of the Garagano Peninsula, the Tremiti Islands is an archipelago with 4 major islands – Capraia, Cretaccio, San Domino, and San Nicolo. Once used as a place for punishment and exile, the islands today are a major Apulian destination attracting over 100,000 visitors in the summer months alone.

The most common way to reach the islands is through the ferry services. Ferries are available from Termoli, Foggia, Vieste, and Peschichi. One can choose between the fast (45 min) and the slow (1 hr 45 min) ferry. Ferry services cost less than €20.

Another option, which is quicker and surprisingly not too expensive either, is the helicopter service! Operating from the Gino Lisa Airport in Foggia, the helicopter flies directly to San Domino Island and costs about €50 in the summer months, but almost half of it during the off-peak season. Once in Tremiti, which is a no-auto zone, one can see most of these small islands on foot and take the water taxi to do island hopping.

San Nicola is where most of the local population resides whereas San Domino Island is the largest and most developed for tourism. Attractions in San Domino include the Rural Village set up in 1935, the Pinewood Road, the Romito Chapel, and the lighthouse. In San Nicola, one can visit the colossal Badia Castle, the Santa Maria Abbey, and the Libyan Cemetery. Other than enjoying the sun-soaked small beaches of these islands, one can take a water taxi to visit the beautiful water caves, namely the Viole Cave, the Blue Marino Cave, and the Rondinelle Cave. Also worth seeing are the stunning bays, the Architiellei rock arches, and the numerous picturesque creeks.

The restaurants and hotels are mostly concentrated in the island of San Domino. Restaurants like the Galeone and Pirata serve seafood and pizza, whereas others like the Torrione and Gabbiano specialize in local Tremitese dishes. Hotels on the island include Gabbiano, Eden, and the San Domino.

Ostuni

Located in the province of Brindisi, the 'White Town' of Ostuni is regarded as one of the most beautiful towns in the Apulian region. The whitewashed Mediterranean arches, cobbled alleys, staircases, and small roads give the town a unique and scenic look that attracts tourists from all across the globe. In fact, during the peak tourist season, the 30,000 town folk are easily outnumbered by the tourist population which is in excess of 100000! In spite of this picturesque man-made monochrome, nature plays a big role to add to the beauty of this hillside town. The red clay, the green top of the olive trees, and azure sky in the background adds to the palette of this Apulian gem.

Unlike many other Apulian cities, Ostuni's growth was under the Norman and Italian rule and not the Romans. Between the 14th and 16th centuries, Ostuni saw the growth of a castle and a medieval town. Today, the remains of this castle, the old town, along with a cathedral are the biggest architectural draws of Ostuni. As the town is only 8 km from the coast, many visitors also take the short trip to the beautiful coast which has retained its natural charm in spite of the heavy foot fall of tourists.

Lecce (Pug Girl, CC BY 2.0)

Barletta-Andria-Trani

The Province of Barletta-Andria-Trani was created in 2009 by separating 10 municipalities from the provinces of Bari and Foggia.

The main cities of this new province are Andria, Barletta, and Trani – all from the province of Bari.

Andria is located about 10 km from the coast and is one of the largest municipalities in the Apulian region. Primarily an agricultural center, the city is famous for its olives, wine, and almonds. Founded sometime around the 10th century, the city became an important seat of administration by the 14th century. It was the residence of choice of

Frederick II, who also gave the town what is today its most popular tourist attraction, a fascinating castle on the outskirts of town. The castle, featured on the Italian one-cent coin, is also listed by UNESCO as a World Heritage Site. Other tourist attractions of Andria include the Ducal Palace, the Communal Palace, and a number of medieval churches, namely, the St Agostino Church, St Francis Church, San Domenico Church, and the Holy Cross Church.

Barletta, located on the coast of the Adriatic, is about 10 km from Andria, and 12 km from Trani. Barletta is one of the oldest inhabited cities in Puglia and has been the witness to many battles over the centuries. One of the tourist highlights of the city is the Colossus of Barletta, the bronze statue of a Roman Emperor. Standing at a height of 4 m, this was the tallest statue in the Late Roman Empire. Other attractions in Barletta include the 10th century Norman Castle, the 12th century Basilica of the Holy Sepulchre, the 13th century Cathedral, and the 11th century San Giacomo Church.

The historic fishing port of Trani grew into prominence between the 11th and 13th centuries. Today, this sleepy town on the Adriatic coast with its landmark seafront cathedral, numerous Romanesque churches and palaces, casual charm, and relaxed atmosphere is a perfect getaway for those looking for a relaxing day trip. The highlight is surely the 12th century cathedral at Piazza Duomo. With its Romanesque style of architecture and its 32-panel engraved bronze doors, it is one of the most beautiful churches in the Apulian region. Nature lovers will love the 19th century public gardens at Villa Comunale, located beside Piazza Plebiscito. Other notable attractions in Trani include the Gothic Palace by the harbor, the Old Fort, the Church of Ognissanti, and the Clock Tower at Via Porta Antica.

Budget Tips

Lecce Plaza (vic15, CC BY 2.0)

Accommodation

Gabbiano

Piazza Belvedere, San Domino
Tremiti Islands
Tel: 0882 4634 10

Located on the picturesque San Domino Island, the Gabbiano hotel is one the best lodging in the Tremiti archipelago. The hotel has arrangements for pick up from the port and it is recommended for those who are carrying extra luggage as Tremiti has no public transport. The hotel has a terrace, fitness room, and a popular restaurant and bar.

Rooms come with a mini bar, hair dryer, AC, and TV. Room rates start from €100 for a double room which includes breakfast.

Martina Franca (Pug Girl, CC BY 2.0)

Eos

Viale Alfieri 11
Lecce 73100
Tel: 0832 2 300 30
http://www.hoteleos.it/

Located about a 10 min walk from the Lecce city center, the Eos hotel is a 3 star property with a relaxed atmosphere and warm hospitality. The hotel has free parking, concierge, and room service. There is an onsite bar.

The spacious ensuite rooms have mini bar, TV, AC, hairdryer, and Wi-Fi (at €10 per hr). Room rate starts from €80 for a double room which includes a buffet breakfast.

Hotel Oriantale

Corso Garibaldi 40
72100 Brindisi
Tel: 0831 5684 51
http://www.hotelorientale.it/index.php?lang=en

Located in the historic city center and just 500 m from the Brindisi Train Station, the Hotel Oriantale is a 4 star hotel with a sleek and modern design. It has free parking, free bikes, and a fitness center. The adjoining lively street has numerous stores, cafes, and restaurants. The hotel has a separate smoking floor for guests.

Rooms have free Wi-Fi, newspaper, coffee, and satellite TV. Room rates, including breakfast, start from €75 for single and €100 for a double room.

Matera (Pug Girl, CC BY 2.0)

Nicolaus Hotel

Via Cardinal A, Ciasca 27
Bari 70124
Tel: 080 5682 111
http://www.nicolaushotels.com/en/our-hotels/nicolaus-hotel

The Nicolaus Hotel is a 4 star property and is located a short drive from the Bari Train Station. On request the hotel provides free shuttle service from the airport. The hotel is equipped with an indoor pool, sauna, Jacuzzi, and fitness center. It has 3 restaurants with one on the terrace on the 14th floor with a sea-view.

Rooms have free Wi-Fi, AC, and satellite TV. Some also have a balcony. Room rates start from €80 and include breakfast.

Hotel Degli Haethey

Via Antonio Esforza 33, 73028 Otranto, Lecce
Tel: 0836 801 548
http://www.hoteldeglihaethey.com/en/

Located very close to the sea, the Degli Haethey is a 4 star hotel in Lecce.

This theme hotel is dedicated to jazz music and has many spaces dedicated to the masters of this genre. There is free parking and free shuttle service. The hotel has a bar, massage center, and fitness center.

The spacious rooms have free Wi-Fi, satellite TV, mini bar, and hair dryer. Room rates start from €100.

Matera (Pug Girl, CC BY 2.0)

Places to Eat

Quinessenza

Via Nigro 37, 76125 Trani
Tel: 0883 880 948
http://www.quintessenzaristorante.it/it/

Equipped with a multilingual staff, excellent service, and of course, delicious food, the Quinessenza is a top rated restaurant in Trani. It serves Mediterranean cuisine. Menu includes salads, various authentic Italian dishes, and dessert. A 7-course set meal is priced at €55. The restaurant also has a very good collection of wine.

Matera Hillside (Pug Girl, CC BY 2.0)

Da Pio

Via Aldo Moro 12, San Domino, Tremiti Islands
Tel: 0882 463 269

Open daily for lunch and dinner, the Da Pio is the ideal place to try
Tremitese cuisine, especially the sea food.

The restaurant has its own fishing boats that bring in fresh catch from the
sea. No wonder the specialty of the restaurant is pasta with lobster. There
is also a wide variety of baked and grilled fish; specially recommended is
the baked fish with potatoes. Entrees are priced from €10.

Alle Due Corti

Corte dei Giugni 1, 73100 Lecce
Tel: 0832 24 22 23
http://www.alleduecortishop.com/alleduecorti/eng/ze_index.htm

Reservation is recommended in this restaurant that serves typical Apulian cuisine. The menu with its Salentine dishes include items like spicy salami, mixed cheese, a variety of pasta, horsemeat in tomato sauce, lamb with artichokes, and many desserts. Main courses range between €9 and €15. It is open Monday to Saturday for lunch and dinner.

Ostuni (Pug Girl, CC BY 2.0)

La Tavernetta

Via Vittorio Emanuele 30
Martina Franca
Tel: 080 430 63 23

Located in the busy Old Town of Martina Franca, the La Tavernetta offers a wide variety of Apulian dishes at a very reasonable price. Most of the dishes are priced under €10. Dishes include typical Italian ones like caprese salads, orecchiette, and spaghetti carbonara. The restaurant is open from Friday to Wednesday during lunch and dinner hours.

Trattoria Cucina Casareccia

Via Costadura 19
73100 Lecce
Tel: 0832 245 178
http://www.lezietrattoria.com/

This restaurant serves authentic Apulian cuisine at a reasonable price. Main dishes cost between €8 and €14. The dishes are cooked with fresh local spices and ingredients. The house specialties are the traditional fish and meat dishes. Specially recommended are the bean puree, potato pie, and beef meatballs.

Ostuni (Pug Girl, CC BY 2.0)

Shopping

Shopping in Bari

Bari is an excellent place to shop for Italian fashion items. The most popular shopping street in the city is Via Sparano which has stores of many famous national and international brands like Furla, Rossetti, Zara, and Sisley. Via Manzoni and Corso Cavour have stores of the slightly cheaper brands. For those hunting for bargain products can go to Via Tammaso or to the Old Town market.

Ostuni (Pug Girl, CC BY 2.0)

Shopping in Lecce

Lecce is known for many traditional arts and crafts and there are many stores all across town where one can find a wide variety of these products. Mostra dell Artigianato on Via Francesco Rubichi sells products made of papier mache, terra cotta, and ceramics. For those looking for wine from the Lecce region can head to Enoteca on Via Cesare Battisti where not can one buy a bottle or two but also taste the wine before buying it.

Shopping in Alberobello & Trulli

The quintessential buy from any souvenir shop in this region are the clay figurines and models.

The handcrafted miniature models of famous buildings and monuments are traditional favorites and a must-buy for almost every tourist. Many of these miniatures are created in the same way as in the ancient times. Trulli is also an ideal place to buy Italian rugs and fabric.

Otranto (JingKe888, CC BY 2.0)

Shopping in Ostuni

There is a wide variety of products to choose from when shopping in Ostuni. Centro Storico has a number of stores, with many selling items aimed at the visiting tourists. Although there are many stores selling jewelry and clothes, the highlight of Ostuni are the ceramic products, which are scattered in many parts of town. If one is visiting on the weekend, the Saturday morning market is a must-visit. Regarded as one of the largest in Italy, the markets sells a variety of items ranging from clothes and accessories to perishable products like fresh farm produce, cheese, fruits, and olive oil.

Shopping in Trani

Trani is popular for selling Italian fabric and clothes. There are a few shopping streets like the Corso Vittorio Emanuele which runs parallel to the coast. Clothing stores on the street include Quadragroup, Nugnes, and Edward. The Delize Pugliese - http://www.deliziepugliesi.com/english/index.html, on Via Maria Pagano is a popular store selling a variety of food products that can be bought for gifts. Products sold in the store include organic honey and flavored oil.

Otranto (Pandemia, CC BY 2.0)

Know Before You Go

Entry Requirements

By virtue of the Schengen agreement, travellers from other countries in the European Union do not need a visa when visiting Italy. Additionally Swiss travellers are also exempt. Visitors from certain other countries such as the USA, Canada, Japan, Israel, Australia and New Zealand do not need visas if their stay in Italy does not exceed 90 days. When entering Italy you will be required to make a declaration of presence, either at the airport, or at a police station within eight days of arrival. This applies to visitors from other Schengen countries, as well as those visiting from non-Schengen countries.

Puglia Coastline (Nouhailler, CC BY-SA 2.0)

Health Insurance

Citizens of other EU countries are covered for emergency health care in Italy. UK residents, as well as visitors from Switzerland are covered by the European Health Insurance Card (EHIC), which can be applied for free of charge. Visitors from non-Schengen countries will need to show proof of private health insurance that is valid for the duration of their stay in Italy (that offers at least €37,500 coverage), as part of their visa application. No special vaccinations are required.

Travelling with Pets

Italy participates in the Pet Travel Scheme (PETS) which allows UK residents to travel with their pets without requiring quarantine upon re-entry. Certain conditions will need to be met. The animal will have to be microchipped and up to date on rabies vaccinations. In the case of dogs, a vaccination against canine distemper is also required by the Italian authorities. When travelling from the USA, your pet will need to be micro-chipped or marked with an identifying tattoo and up to date on rabies vaccinations. An EU Annex IV Veterinary Certificate for Italy will need to be issued by an accredited veterinarian. On arrival in Italy, you can apply for an EU pet passport to ease your travel in other EU countries.

Puglia Coastline From Peschici to Mattinata (Nouhailler, CC BY-SA 2.0)

Airports

Fiumicino – Leonardo da Vinci International Airport (FCO) is one of the busiest airports in Europe and the main international airport of Italy. It is located about 35km southwest of the historical quarter of Rome. Terminal 5 is used for trans-Atlantic and international flights, while Terminals 1, 2 and 3 serve mainly for domestic flights and medium haul flights to other European destinations. Before Leonardo da Vinci replaced it, the **Ciampino–G. B. Pastine International Airport** (CIA) was the main international airport servicing Rome and Italy. It is one of the oldest airports in the country still in use. Although it declined in importance, budget airlines such as Ryanair boosted its air traffic in recent years. The airport is used by Wizz Air, V Bird, Helvetic, Transavia Airlines, Sterling, Ryanair, Thomsonfly, EasyJet, Air Berlin, Hapag-Lloyd Express and

Carpatair.

Milan Malpensa Airport (MXP) is the largest of the three airports serving the city of Milan. Located about 40km northwest of Milan's city center, it connects travellers to the regions of Lombardy, Piedmont and Liguria. **Milan Linate Airport** (LIN) is Milan's second international airport. **Venice Marco Polo Airport** (VCE) provides access to the charms of Venice. **Olbia Costa Smeralda Airport** (OLB) is located near Olbia, Sardinia. Main regional airports are **Guglielmo Marconi Airport** (BLQ), an international airport servicing the region of Bologna, **Capodichino Airport** at Naples (NAP), **Pisa International Airport** (PSA), formerly Galileo Galilei Airport, the main airport serving Tuscany, **Sandro Pertini Airport** near Turin (TRN), **Cristoforo Colombo** in Genoa (GOA), **Punta Raisi Airport** in Palermo (PMO), **Vincenzo Bellini Airport** in Catania (CTA) and **Palese Airport** in Bari (BRI).

Airlines

Alitalia is the flag carrier and national airline of Italy. It has a subsidiary, Alitalia CityLiner, which operates short-haul regional flights. Air Dolomiti is a regional Italian based subsidiary of of the Lufthansa Group. Meridiana is a privately owned airline based at Olbia in Sardinia.

Fiumicino - Leonardo da Vinci International Airport serves as the main hub for Alitalia, which has secondary hubs at Milan Linate and Milan Malpensa Airport. Alitalia CityLiner uses Fiumicino – Leonardo da Vinci International Airport as main hub and has secondary hubs at Milan-Linate, Naples and Trieste. Fiumicino – Leonardo da Vinci International Airport is also one of two primary hubs used by the budget Spanish airline Vueling. Milan Malpensa Airport is one of the largest bases for the British budget airline EasyJet. Venice Airport serves as an Italian base for the Spanish budget airline, Volotea, which provides connections mainly to other destinations in Europe. Olbia Costa Smeralda Airport (OLB), located near Olbia, Sardinia is the primary base of Meridiana, a private Italian Airline in partnership with Air Italia and Fly Egypt.

Puglia, Country House Cefalicchio in Bari (Toprural, CC BY-SA 2.0)

Currency

Italy's currency is the Euro. It is issued in notes in denominations of €500, €200, €100, €50, €20, €10 and €5. Coins are issued in denominations of €2, €1, 50c, 20c, 10c, 5c, 2c and 1c.

Banking & ATMs

Using ATMs or Bancomats, as they are known in Italy, to withdraw money is simple if your ATM card is compatible with the MasterCard/Cirrus or Visa/Plus networks. There is a €250 limit on daily withdrawals. Italian machines are configured for 4-digit PIN numbers, although some machines will be able to handle longer PIN numbers. Bear in mind some Bancomats can run out of cash over weekends and that the more remote villages may not have adequate banking facilities so plan ahead.

Spiaggia Del Gargano (Roby Ferrari, CC BY-SA 2.0)

Credit Cards

Credit cards are valid tender in most Italian businesses. While Visa and MasterCard are accepted universally, most tourist oriented businesses also accept American Express and Diners Club. Credit cards issued in Europe are smart cards that that are fitted with a microchip and require a PIN for each transaction. This means that a few ticket machines, self-service vendors and other businesses may not be configured to accept the older magnetic strip credit cards. Do remember to advise your bank or credit card company of your travel plans before leaving.

Tourist Taxes

Tourist tax varies from city to city, as each municipality sets its own rate. The money is collected by your accommodation and depends on the standard of accommodation. A five star establishment will levy a higher amount than a four star or three star establishment. You can expect to pay somewhere between €1 and €7 per night, with popular destinations like Rome, Venice, Milan and Florence charging a higher overall rate. In some regions, the rate is also adjusted seasonally. Children are usually exempt until at least the age of 10 and sometimes up to the age of 18. In certain areas, disabled persons and their companions also qualify for discounted rates. Tourist tax is payable directly to the hotel or guesthouse before the end of your stay.

Trani (Pandemia, CC BY 2.0)

Reclaiming VAT

If you are not from the European Union, you can claim back VAT (Value Added Tax) paid on your purchases in Italy. The VAT rate in Italy is 21 percent and this can be claimed back on your purchases if certain conditions are met. The merchant needs to be partnered with a VAT refund program. This will be indicated if the shop displays a Tax Free sign. The shop assistant will fill out a form for reclaiming VAT. When you submit this at the airport, you will receive your refund.

Tipping Policy

If your bill includes the phrase coperto e servizio, that means that a service charge or tip is already included. Most waiting staff in Italy are salaried workers, but if the service is excellent, a few euros extra would be appreciated.

Mobile Phones

Most EU countries, including Italy use the GSM mobile service. This means that most UK phones and some US and Canadian phones and mobile devices will work in Italy. While you could check with your service provider about coverage before you leave, using your own service in roaming mode will involve additional costs. The alternative is to purchase an Italian SIM card to use during your stay in Italy.

Italy has four mobile networks. They are TIM, Wind, Vodafone and Tre (3) and they all provide pre-paid services. TIM offers two tourist options, both priced at €20 (+ €10 for the SIM card) with a choice of two packages - 2Gb data, plus 200 minutes call time or internet access only with a data allowance of 5Gb. Vodafone, Italy's second largest network offers a Vodafone Holiday package including SIM card for €30. They also offer the cheapest roaming rates. Wind offers an Italian Tourist pass for €20 which includes 100 minutes call time and 2Gb data and can be extended with a restart option for an extra €10.

To purchase a local SIM card, you will need to show your passport or some other form of identification and provide your residential details in Italy. By law, SIM registration is required prior to activation. Most Italian SIM cards expire after a 90 day period of inactivity. When dialling internationally, remember to use the (+) sign and the code of the country you are connecting to.

Dialling Code

The international dialling code for Italy is +39.

Emergency Numbers

Police: 113

Fire: 115
Ambulance: 118
MasterCard: 800 789 525
Visa: 800 819 014

Public Holidays

1 January: New Year's Day (Capodanno)
6 January: Day of the Epiphany (Epifania)
March-April: Easter Monday (Lunedì dell'Angelo or Pasquetta)
25 April: Liberation Day (Festa della Liberazione)
1 May: International Worker's Day (Festa del Lavoro / Festa dei Lavoratori)
2 June: Republic Day (Festa della Repubblica)
15 August: Assumption Day (Ferragosto / Assunta)
1 November: All Saints Day (Tutti i santi / Ognissanti)
8 December: Immaculate Conception (Immacolata Concezione / Immacolata)
25 December: Christmas Day (Natale)
26 December: St Stephen's Day (Santo Stefano)

A number of Saints days are observed regionally throughout the year.

Time Zone

Italy falls in the Central European Time Zone. This can be calculated as Greenwich Mean Time/Coordinated Universal Time (GMT/UTC) +2; Eastern Standard Time (North America) -6; Pacific Standard Time (North America) -9.

Daylight Savings Time

Clocks are set forward one hour on 29 March and set back one hour on 25 October for Daylight Savings Time.

School Holidays

The academic year begins in mid September and ends in mid June. The summer holiday is from mid June to mid September, although the exact times may vary according to region. There are short breaks around Christmas and New Year and also during Easter. Some regions such as Venice and Trentino have an additional break during February for the carnival season.

Trading Hours

Trading hours for the majority of shops are from 9am to 12.30pm and then again from 3.30pm to 7.30pm, although in some areas, the second shift may be from 4pm to 8pm instead. The period between 1pm and 4pm is known in Italy as the *riposo*. Large department shops and malls tend to be open from 9am to 9pm, from Monday to Saturday. Post offices are open from 8.30am to 1.30pm from Monday to Saturday. Most shops and many restaurants are closed on Sundays. Banking hours are from 8.30am to 1.30pm and then again from 3pm to 4pm, Monday to Friday. Most restaurants are open from noon till 2.30pm and then again from 7pm till 11pm or midnight, depending on the establishment. Nightclubs open around 10pm, but only liven up after midnight. Closing times vary, but will generally be between 2am and 4am. Museum hours vary, although major sights tend to be open continuously and often up to 7.30pm. Many museums are closed on Mondays.

Driving Laws

The Italians drive on the right hand side of the road. A driver's licence from any of the European Union member countries is valid in Italy. Visitors from non-EU countries will require an International Driving Permit that must remain current throughout the duration of their stay in Italy.

The speed limit on Italy's autostrade is 130km per hour and 110km per hour on main extra-urban roads, but this is reduced by 20km to 110km and 90km respectively in rainy weather. On secondary extra-urban roads, the speed limit is 90km per hour; on urban highways, it is 70km per hour and on urban roads, the speed limit is 50km per hour. You are not allowed to drive in the ZTL or Limited Traffic Zone (or *zona traffico limitato* in Italian) unless you have a special permit.

Visitors to Italy are allowed to drive their own non-Italian vehicles in the country for a period of up to six months. After this, they will be required to obtain Italian registration with Italian licence plates. Italy has very strict laws against driving under the influence of alcohol. The blood alcohol limit is 0.05 and drivers caught above the limit face penalties such as fines of up to €6000, confiscation of their vehicles, suspension of their licenses and imprisonment of up to 6 months. Breathalyzer tests are routine at accident scenes.

Drinking Laws

The legal drinking age in Italy is 16. While drinking in public spaces is allowed, public drunkenness is not tolerated. Alcohol is sold in bars, wine shops, liquor stores and grocery shops.

Smoking Laws

In 2005, Italy implemented a policy banning smoking from public places such as bars, restaurants, nightclubs and working places, limiting it to specially designated smoking rooms. Further legislation banning smoking from parks, beaches and stadiums is being explored.

Electricity

Electricity: 220 volts
Frequency: 50 Hz

Italian electricity sockets are compatible with the Type L plugs, a plug that features three round pins or prongs, arranged in a straight line. An alternate is the two-pronged Type C Euro adaptor. If travelling from the USA, you will need a power converter or transformer to convert the voltage from 220 to 110, to avoid damage to your appliances. The latest models of many laptops, camcorders, mobile phones and digital cameras are dual-voltage with a built in converter.

Tourist Information (TI)

There are tourist information (TI) desks at each of the terminals of the Leonardo da Vinci International Airport, as well as interactive Information kiosks with the latest touch-screen technology. In Rome, the tourist office can be found at 5 Via Parigi, near the Termini Station and it is identified as APT, which stands for Azienda provinciale del Turismo. Free maps and brochures of current events are available from tourist kiosks.

Several of the more tourist-oriented regions of Italy offer tourist cards that include admission to most of the city's attractions. While these cards are not free, some offer great value for money. A variety of tourism apps are also available online.

Food & Drink

Pasta is a central element of many typically Italian dishes, but there are regional varieties and different types of pasta are matched to different sauces. Well known pasta dishes such as lasagne and bolognaise originated in Bologna. Stuffed pasta is popular in the northern part of Italy, while the abundance of seafood and olives influences southern Italian cuisine. As far as pizza goes, the Italians differentiate between the thicker Neapolitan pizza and the thin crust Roman pizza, as well as white pizza, also known as focaccia and tomato based pizza. Other standards include minestrone soup, risotto, polenta and a variety of cheeses, hams, sausages and salamis. If you are on a budget, consider snacking on stuzzichini with a few drinks during happy hour which is often between 7 and 9pm. The fare can include salami, cheeses, cured meat, mini pizzas, bread, vegetables, pastries or pate. In Italy, Parmesan refers only to cheese originating from the area surrounding Parma. Favorites desserts include tiramisu or Italian gelato.

Italians enjoy relaxing to aperitifs before they settle down to a meal and their favorites are Campari, Aperol or Negroni, the famous Italian cocktail. Wine is enjoyed with dinner. Italy is particularly famous for its red wines. The best known wine regions are Piedmont, which produces robust and dry reds, Tuscany and Alto Adige, where Alpine soil adds a distinctive acidity. After the meal, they settle down to a glass of limoncello, the country's most popular liqueur, or grappa, which is distilled from grape seeds and stems, as digestive. Other options in this class include a nut liqueur, nocino, strawberry based Fragolino Veneto or herbal digestives like gineprino, laurino or mirto. Italians are also fond of coffee. Espresso is drunk through throughout the day, but cappuccino is considered a morning drink. The most popular beers in Italy are Peroni and Moretti.

Websites

http://vistoperitalia.esteri.it/home/en

This is the website of the Consulate General of Italy. Here you can look up whether you will need a visa and also process your application online.

http://www.italia.it/en/home.html

The official website of Italian tourism

http://www.italia.it/en/useful-info/mobile-apps.html

Select the region of your choice to download a useful mobile app to your phone.

http://www.italylogue.com/tourism

http://italiantourism.com/index.html

http://www.reidsitaly.com/

http://wikitravel.org/en/Italy

https://www.summerinitaly.com/

http://www.accessibleitalianholiday.com/

Planning Italian vacations around the needs of disabled tourists.

Printed in Great Britain
by Amazon

82316738R00031